Maiden Rock

by
Peter MLADINIC

Maiden Rock

Cover Art: Henry Stanton

Back Cover Portrait: [BLANK]

Book Design by: Henry Stanton, UnCollected Press

UnCollected Press
8320 Main Street, 2nd Floor
Ellicott City, MD 21043

For more books by UnCollected Press:
www.therawartreview.com

First Edition 2024
ISBN: 9798-9905585-5-7

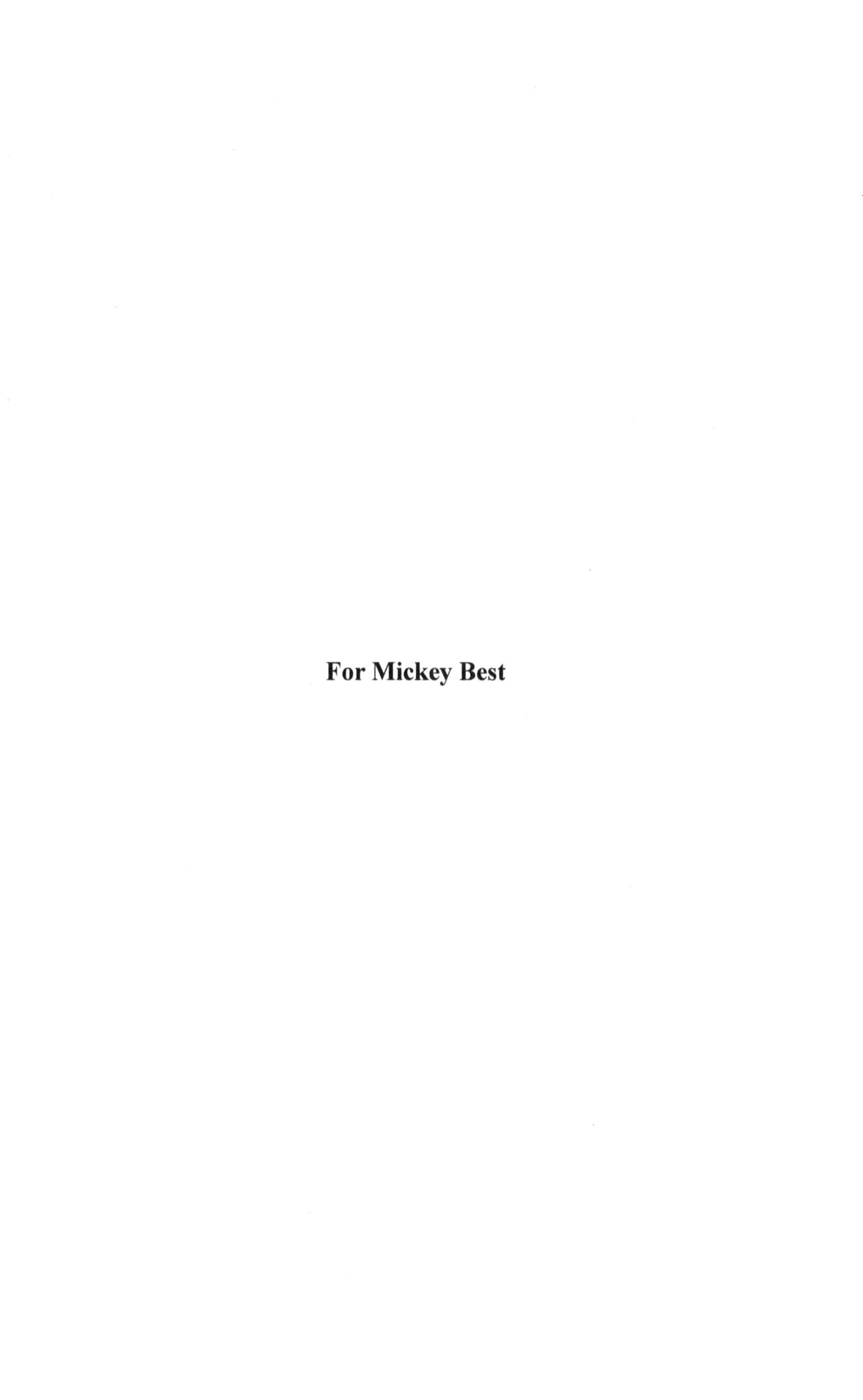

For Mickey Best

Contents

Maiden Rock

White clouds in a blue sky,
a two-story wooden house on
a hill
Saturday afternoon—
Are you offended by the
clouds' words,
their voices I'd quiet
but high as they are they
cannot hear?
Come back. Tell me
their names.

Our Friend's Daughter

Adolescents are children. I'm not like one of
these commentators who say the young
man barged into the Springfield
Target with an AK-47 and started shooting,
when talking about a 17-year-old child,
and where did he get the assault riffle?

But I am a war veteran. I know a mother
in Uvalde, Texas. The Springfield Target
could just as well be the El Paso Walmart.
Could just as well be a church, a school,
a post office. *Gun Crazy* is a good movie.
To see it, you'd have to rent or buy it.

But this wasn't a movie, just a memory.
A dinner outdoors with friends in Taos. Bob,
an airline pilot from Florida, AK-47 owner
because, besides flying, he's also in law
enforcement, says he asked a lawyer friend,
also an AK-47 owner, Would you give up

your AK-47 if it meant bringing our friend's
daughter back? She died in the Stoneman
Douglas High School shooting. If giving up
your weapon meant bringing her back
to life, would you do it? No, it wouldn't end
there, with the assault rifle, soon, they'd be

taking all our guns. The lawyer may just as
well have said the shootings wouldn't end.
Yes, the criminals find a way. I understand.
But what about fewer guns, fewer killings?
When I came back from Vietnam people
asked, Did you kill anyone? Gun crazy USA

Australia

There was the young Long Island woman,
somewhere close by her brother, her dad,
and we're bunched by the bar, the deck
with the bandstand and line for burgers.
We're at canopy covered bar, sunset at sea
end of cruise booze merry. She's tan, long
wavy hair, aquiline nose. He leans, his kiss
barely touches her mouth. She didn't like it.

Days earlier, smoking deck, I got chummy
with an Australian, the cruise had lots of
Aussies, is that okay, not offensive? She
from Melbourne, an out of a storybook city
on the ocean, had had a daughter, a babe
that died while being babysat, and a pal,
cruising with her, Marlboros on the table.
She took one from the box. So, Your friend...

Didn't ask, Is he married? I was let down
she preferred him over me. You think he's
better looking than me? He's married, I'm
thinking. Then her pal joins us, dark hair,
taller, bigger. I looked and thought the pal
a girl I could kiss. Forget Ms. Melbourne.
She preferred My pal, taller than I, my pal
of the I'm on my fifth rum unwanted kiss.

Pop Culture Elegy

Cornell Gunter

What America does with its singers,
it takes them out and shoots them.
Full of bullet holes they're good and silent,
not a note. It keeps them from singing
truths it can't bear to hear. Cornell,
shot in a car parked, a street in Vegas,
assailant unknown, cross-dressed,
which isn't a crime. With the Flairs,
the Coasters his tenor rang too true.
A bullet in a parked car. Same for Dyke,
invented funk, Dyke and the Blazers.
It's what America does with singers.

Sal Mineo

His absence among the most notable
in American cinema: the community lined
the tracks, the flat open car pulls up
with the flag draped coffin of their Angel.
Every eye fixated on the big screen's
earth meets sky horizon. West Texas,
Angel Obergon the soldier who died for us
the poor, the rich is home, is no more.

Judy Tyler

No one saw Elvis cry. He cried
on hearing of your fatal auto
accident near Rock River. You
and the King had finished *Jailhouse Rock*.

On Howdy Doody, Buffalo Bob said
girls and boys, here's

Princess Summerfall Winterspring. Your cue.
You playfully booted Clarabell's rear,
his horn-like nose tooted
and extolled the benefits of Wonder Bread
to Phineas T.

The commute from Teaneck
into the City, the auditions and work
paid off, got you in Elvis's movie.

Christina

John said, "When I talk to Christina
I feel I'm reminding her of her illness,"
that the ovarian cancer that was more
than ovarian cancer is more

than anyone who is not her
or like her can imagine. Not even
her son and husband.
If John calls, it's a reminder. So he

leaves her alone, which maybe Christina
doesn't want. I too don't want to call and
have that like a bell ringing inside her.
If I call, will she feel forced to talk about it?

The turquoise waters off Bermuda
or the Friday night I sat across from her,
a towel over my face and head after
my fifth martini in her home—

I could talk about anything
but the thing. Cancer. We say "I feel
your pain" about the loss of a pet
or an aunt one hasn't seen in years.

My call is good timing.
No white blood cells, immunology,
a new doctor. She has to go.
She has to say goodbye

to the dog next door they're taking
to the vet to euthanize.
But she's doing okay, better than
last October.

About That Sunday at the Audubon Ballroom

1.

You bite the hand that feeds you,
someone's going to chop off your hand,
which is what happened to Malcolm
that Sunday afternoon in the Audubon.
The sawed-off shotgun not in my hand.
The blast of pellets that struck the heart
of the hypocrite, once second in command,
wasn't mine, though, yes, I was there.
William X Bradley, from Newark's Mosque
25, played baseball in high school,
served prison time for threatening lives
of three people and took my last breath
in 2018. I was there for Elijah, my heavenly
father, the Honorable Elijah Muhammad
against whom the hypocrite blasphemed
from a podium that Sunday afternoon.
When they carry Thomas Hagan,
holding his legs and arms, chest facing
sidewalk like they're ready to toss him,
you see me walk by in the film footage,
stocky, dark-complected, nonchalant
buttoning my topcoat, a white
pamphlet sticking out its side pocket,
but not me unarmed in the Ford Falcon
riding shotgun through the tunnel, flying
home to Mosque 25, as the coroner
pronounces Malcolm dead. I didn't do it.
I was a soldier of Islam, a messenger,
years later a man dying from emphysema
in a hospital bed. Long live Islam.
Death to the hypocrite, cut out his tongue!
Cut off the hand of anyone who speaks
against who gave me life, my heavenly
father. But no, my hand didn't whip out

the shotgun, that was another soldier.

2.

He was not an enemy of white people.
In speeches he condemned them,
but look at the contexts of the speeches
of Malcolm X, an enemy of injustice,
whatever colors or skin injustice wore.
He thought race important, and talked
passionately, lucidly about segregation,
unequal treatment, race-based beatings,
burnings, lynchings of blacks by whites
and more. Who killed him? Some say
white people. Did he hate white people?
He was the consummate anti-racist.
Changing and embracing his changes
he was not dogmatic. He often smiled.
His brief life made for a better world.

Black Beard, White Dog

In the dark morning I walk to work,
past your house. It is 1975.
Your beard is black. You sleep.
Engulfed by gentle oblivion
the white dog sleeps. The white cat
in a window looks out at the dark
street. My work is to live.
In your dream you throw a stick
into water, the white dog
fetches my life and brings me to you.

Elvis's Pompadour

I can't see Tricky Dick or JFK like that,
clean-cut young man, doing his patriotic
part far from Sun Records West Memphis

and the Shreveport stage where hips and
a prop-guitar rock him into idol spotlight.
Later, in a photo with Nixon at the White House—

I've enlisted Elvis to help me fight drugs—
it hides ears that had listened to "Mystery
Train" at Sun and heard possibilities.

By the time of the White House photo
the face is beginning to bloat. His hair
not shoulder-length but long, his eyes—

he's a drug-addled Vegas Elvis, the King,
sure, but a far cry from the hip shaker
idol of Louisiana Hayride. "That's

Alright Mama" frenzies teens. Behind
Elvis, a pink stage jacket. His brow's
dissenting cowlick the right touch.

Central Air

It's undeniable,
wherever you are is the center of the world
I've come to, to admire the distance
between us.

*

Pretend you're married, your marriage is
falling apart.
In the courtyard of a one story school
you find a hundred dollar bill.

*

There was a plastic palm tree in the corner,
the television was turned off.
You're boring, you said. Decades later
I read Boring Is the New Interesting.

*

Before central air you were fortunate
enough to have electricity, and put a plug
in a socket. A fan cooled the corner
where you sat reading *Readers Digest*.

*

Turtles with orange shells wouldn't bite,
Snappers with black jagged edged shells
would. Small green turtles in pet shops,
you took three home. They swam
with tiny claws in a round plastic dish.
All you had to do was practically look at one
and it died.

*

Youth is foolish. He held you by
the ankles as you upside down dangled
over a banister, above a flight of stairs.
Instead of trying to pull you to safety
I laughed.

The Dog No One Wants

I'm not talking about a Yorkie, a teacup
Chihuahua or any of those fancy breeds,
but the dog at the shelter no one wants,

and not because it bites, stinks, sheds.
Only the workers know of this dog's pros
and cons, even they hardly know,

inundated as they are. Nothing
in this medium-sized dog stands out.
It's overlooked by people. Who needs it?

Just go in and say give me the dog
no one wants, the one no one notices.
They come in, look, walk out with a dog

to care for. Care for that, go against
the grain. Be different, after all you are
different; there's only one you. That dog

most overlooked, that's been there longest,
that's the one, the fit companion
for the needy, caring person you are.

Mantle and Mays

If I could touch what touches everything,
if I could talk to the animals, if I could
remember the Bronx of 1953 as well as you,
the Polo Grounds would my memory, one
we shared, you in stands, the Say Hey Kid
in center, across the river, in center Mick.
His glove like Willie's catches the high pop.

I think of base paths, a batter's box, a dash
third to home. Mantle for speed, power,
Mays for all around everything in the Polo
Grounds, you remember sitting in stands
and I vaguely seeing Mantle but more so
an old man's eye bloodied by a line drive
hit off, say, Brooks Robinson's bat that day

the Yanks hosted Baltimore, Mick figurine-
small way out in center, but step into
the batter's box, cousin, as the Mick did
and the Say Hey Kid, to touch the width
and breadth of what touches all, everything.
New York at Mantle's fingertips, New York
in the pocket of the glove of a kid, Willie

Mays from cotton-field Alabama, Mick
from dustbowl Oklahoma, and you from
greenery of Dumont, the country it was
then, to ride in a Buick across the GW,
step into shadows tall brick walls, courtyard
guarded by stone lions and gargoyles
on ledges and with strength of your eight
year old arms open thick, black-glossed
double doors, high on a hill. So many

cobbled hills, down to the wide Concourse,
sprawl of shops on Fordham, canopies,
the RKO marquee, all the while brick walls
burnished red, brown, light tan of five,
six story buildings. The hand sets a potted

begonia on a fire escape, no more than dust
today, that in '53 when baseball was king,
joined its other hand to clap a storm
for Mays or Mantle. Look at the tiny curls
of blond hairs on his powerful forearm!
A child might have said to himself to herself,
I love Mickey Mantle, or Willie knocks it

out of the park for me, every time. To come
from whatever he was seeing, cotton under
a big sky, Stars Fell on Alabama, uphill,
and in broad light feel something like God's
hand (if I could touch what touches
everything) on his shoulder and hear a voice
say Willie, or Mick, this is yours, all of it.

Mourners at the Mound

Our goodbyes are for him, not you,
that white wreath, for him
for him, our black dress,
the hole you've toppled into, dug for him.
Your cry to the dead, I'm here,
sounds joyful. Are you drunk?

Your bulk rattles the coffin you stand on.
Please respect his young widow.
A white handkerchief dabs her veiled eyes.
She looks down at him in his coffin,
at you in your skin. Respect God in heaven,
beyond the white clouds
in today's bluest sky, Cantinflas,
cease giving death your fleshy finger.

You shame our solemnity
in *El bolero de Raquel.*
You are blind to all but the sky,
deaf to our collective
You're not supposed to. This hole
is for the dead, we are here for him, not you.
What are you doing? Are you drunk?

We said, "Lay the wreath gently,
keep still as a stone."
How you struggle to climb,
your fingers clutching dirt the dead needs.
Get out! Ah, you don't hear,
busy as you are being alive.

Other Nights

The shop teacher told you you'd end up
being a factory worker, but you died
before the dream could be fulfilled.
Paul, I've worked in a factory.
One morning I was counting boxes of meat
in the freezer. This woman's face came before me.
It was peaceful, and I've known other nights.

I desire teenage girls in Glencoe, autumn
afternoon drives along Sheridan Road.
Why am I so afraid of being alone?
Have I ever had an orgasm at the same time
that my lover has had an orgasm?
Sex is all, and all to good to be true.
That's what the doctor said, that afternoon
I didn't call you back from the dead
to cry for my life in the waiting room.

I make love to three women in five days.
Señor Blues is what they call me.
Each time I plunge into my loneliness
I dream of a factory.
Twelve years ago we hitchhiked
past the spot where you'd be underground.

We rode shoulder to shoulder on a bus
to have our pictures taken
by an older man living in a lonelier city.
I knew the dark, thick skin of your body,
your uncircumcised penis, the tone of your
voice in a closeness as intimate as love,
and you used to think I was beautiful.

Fist

In Okinawa I made a fist
and my fingers stuck together
that stop over night
my one stop before Danang,
between two worlds,

the flag burning, tear-gas
U.S. and the Vietnam rat-tat-tat
automatic fire, the LBJ
How many kids…and the sandbag
fortified bunkers. Didn't

see anyone die, only the dead.
In Okinawa, planes
on the runway, the air thicker
than Danang's.

The smell of napalm,
how real for some.
I stood holding a metal tray
in a chow line, slept
in a top bunk, spit-shined boots
so their tips were mirrors.

Snug

In a tent
close space between you and the ground
for warmth. A sleeping bag and under it
layered blankets, a quilt for softness—you'll
be warm as I was that New Year's Eve,
no cold air between what I was on and in.

When I unzipped the bag I dressed quick
and stepped out, 2003, high desert, Taurus
Mesa. Five above zero. A fire of mesquite
blazing, a path lined by rocks led to a rim.
Over the canyon crows flew, their gurgles
like bubbles in an office water cooler.

Becoming Invisible

They moved from city to suburbs. They were
lost, gobbled up, in some dark downstairs
apartment, all you could see were walls.
It was like they'd stopped living, so much

a part of the city they were, and where they
moved wasn't desolate, a little city, but not
theirs of five-story brick walls, cobbled hills.
I see his long coat and fedora, her pillbox

hat with the little veil. You opened a window
looked out at other windows, fire escapes,
brick walls across the street. All that
was gone when they made the move, his

suspenders, the scar from her operation.
This new place it was like they weren't there.

At the Cross

Somebody's elsewhere has an allure
my nimble fingers want to touch:
Luna street, an upstairs room, Rosalina,

on her thigh a dagger tattoo, across it
the name Miguel scrolled crudely,
the dagger's thrust impossible to miss.

No teardrops fell, no blood dripped,
I didn't stop to count, my half hour, times
she broke Miguel's heart and he, hers.

A black ink cross, under skin blood and bone.
I placed a ten in her palm that afternoon.
Nine years later one night at crossroads

someone hurled a bottle out a tavern door,
I failed to hear the missile splinter.
My Colt's Firestones skirted the shards

with ease, in light traffic, the night very cold,
the shards sharp as a tattooed blade
on a human thigh, in my rear-view winter trees.

The tavern on the corner to my left, my Colt's
shift four off the floor. From out the door
a beer bottle sailed into the future,

my elsewhere: minister Gary's office,
on his desk a Bible, on the wall a cross.
He'd played football on a university team.

Brother, I appreciate your strong hands,
kind words, your heart of the true believer.
Pray for Rosalina, for Miguel, for the knife

pierced through his two-syllable name,
(scripture's living word etched on her thigh),
and for a drunk who hurled a beer bottle

into a street, but not for me,
a man with no life but this life, no Christ.
Before my eyes a cross on paid for flesh;

a quiet, frigid night. Somebody's hand
hurls a bottle out a door. In my rearview
light traffic, blind luck shields me from harm.

Message in a Bottle

I took a green bouquet in my left hand
to the ocean. Ocean flowers,
green roses for your green eyes, Mother.

Take my imperfect love bundle, Mother
who rocked me in arms, as I slept,
whose body vessel brought me this shore.

Carry me on nothing to fear,
take this me-dream green destiny of forget
into your bosom's roses, ghost,
sky flame, ship minuscule on the horizon
of boarded glass.

Where ocean and years hover,
plums drop from branches,
near a window a white cloth's gold crumbs
leave no trace
at all. Your hands' oblivion knuckles clouds.
The sea's drowning hand waves far out.
I think it time, retaliation, the eyes in a face
of sand, the answer that is and is not.

I fling feebly to your vast
wave crested nothing, ashes. Kisses
of milk-box near steps
cloud the curved bottle's message:
the all of a corner's broom, April showers.

Roses of the sea lie on the ocean floor.
Apples fall from eternity's green branches.

Lakes

He's at a lake and sees this guy beating
a puppy with the chain of a leash, tells him
to stop; the guy takes his cell (he's calling
911), throws it in the lake, threatens to beat
him up, he's eighty years old, this is in North
Dakota, where he retired from practicing
dentistry years ago, lives with his second
wife, and loves their three dogs and one cat.

When we met he was in dental school. We
had a laugh when Amanda (his first wife)
said her father said, I hope those protesters
aren't disrupting (protester) Tom's studies.
We met in Wilson Library's smoking room,
where they were non-smokers. I knew her
better than him. She had long wavy hair,
liked to laugh; he drove a gray VW bug.

Our smoking room circle rippled wider,
into cafes, movie theaters, house parties.
One of us, Brian, became an MD, I was best
man at his and Theresa's wedding; he, tall,
blond; she, short, Japanese American from
Chicago. I lost touch with them, and Steve,
Colleen, and Marty. One night Amanda
and I in the bug drove out to Lake Harriet

in the dead of night, looked around, nothing
more. Early one night a few years later she
came to my apartment, by that time, she
and Tom had split up. She sensed I wanted
her, I could sense her edginess as she left.
I'd never wanted to sleep with her when she
was Tom's wife, but I did that night. By then,
our circle broken up, I'd lived near Lake of

the Isles, in the top half of a house where
Kate found a dead mouse in the refrigerator,
I lived with her and her younger brother for
a year. Lake of the Isles is in the Mary Tyler
Moore Show, Mary on a tree-lined path in
winter is how it starts. I think they are Dutch
elms. Tom would likely know. A dentist, he's
scientific, specific, likes steam engines,

and loves his pets, which is our bond today,
pets, animals. We haven't seen each other
in forty plus years, same with Amanda,
his ex, who likes flowers. When he told me,
not directly, but posted on Facebook
about the guy beating the pup, I wanted
to go up there and put my arms around him.
He was shaken up. Such a good man.

I don't know why we lost touch all that time.
When we started talking again Tom had
already retired. Like me, he misses
Lake Calhoun, which I bicycled to; Harriet,
where I walked and one night I saw the poet
Charles Rakoski; and Lake of the Isles.
What happened to the sick dog beater?
Tom's not one to let something like that go.

The Difference Between A and Z

When A talks to people she uses their
names, Z doesn't; that's it right there,
that's the heart of it. Both are beauties.
I'm sure in Z there's a soul, a garden.
Her tattoos, her back, her chest, an arm,
a leg are like ivy climbing a wall. One
a script: I love you to the moon. Maybe
you is a sister, or a big love from the past,

a man, his name whispers in the dark.
A, no tattoos, pale but not too pale skin
unblemished, long, straight, very dark
brown hair. Noticeably taller of the two,
she always calls people by their names.
And she doesn't wear a nose ring, nor
does she have piercing an eyebrow
a safety pin, nor a stud near a lower lip.

She's clean. Which is not to say Z isn't,
only, with your blonde hair pulled up
showing your perfect neck, why don't you
once in a blue moon speak my name?
I think it comes down to breeding. A
must have had good breeding. I think
when a person speaks to you and uses
your name…Z teaches. You think she'd

know the importance of that, of speaking a person's name when talking, or texting or in a letter. Do people write letters anymore? I'm not thinking of these, Dear Reese Johnson, we write to inform you you've been accepted at Monmouth Teacher's College bureaucratic affairs. But a letter from one friend to another.

Z's hiding something is what Dorrie said when I told her about this blonde woman she doesn't know, and I know only a little. But I know her better than I know A. At, let's call it, The Crematorium, I see A walking into a room, standing in a corner or, in the lobby, staring out a window. She's breathtaking, pleasant to be near.

Joe

I didn't see Joe in the hospital, telling Millie
he didn't want to die. In our kitchen
at a table, and up the hill getting out of his
car in his driveway. A big man. But when
a kid he'd had this kidney illness wasn't
taken care of, as it could be with today's
technology, and it caught up with him.

He left a young boy and girl, and Millie.
I was too young to go to his funeral, I
imagine, though, Doug and Robin, his kids,
younger than I, were there.
I saw his frame get thin.

In Memory of Major Marie Rossi-Cayton

You love a beautiful sky.
She did too, the first American woman
to die in the Persian Gulf War.
She wasn't in combat when her Chinook
went down. I think of her bravery, sacrifice,
honor we bestow on those with no hands
to hold it, as if it were a folded flag.
She was unborn

when I was in fourth grade.
Her brother sat up front, wore the white shirt
green tie I wore, the girls green jumpers.
She too loved the sky
with a love that got her to be part of war.
I stood in a corner a half hour up front,
I faced the wall.
I was ordered there and obeyed.

You're a girl who loves a beautiful sky.
One morning I sat in your father's office
and he, the Dean of Students suggested
I apologize to students
for having lost my temper in class.
I don't recall my exact words, they
wouldn't be quiet. I used the F word,
up front, beside myself.

Your dad didn't mandate, but clearly said
an apology was in order. He said it
in a nice way, understood my side,
which didn't excuse my out of control.
I did a few things wrong back then,
but I went back to class and apologized.
What became of the brother of the pilot
I don't know, but his younger sister's story
is part of his town's, also our nation's.

I barely knew you that day I sat across your
dad's desk. He listened well. I recall my
silence that half hour in the corner,
the teacher's Roman nose, the brother
a round teddy bear of a boy in a white shirt,
a green necktie. Major Rossi-Cayton
smiles in her uniform of death.

The Bridge of Love

Do you remember, entity out of time,
my Run, Jesse, run, echo of the Chicago
reverend's late 80s presidential campaign?
Run, Jesse! Don't let those birds, yellow
breasted kites, the bush you were in,
don't let them get you! The summer night
you hobbled across the pond's footbridge,
arch of wood slats, Harry MacAdams Park.

No one can take your place, but one has,
a dark four-legged bitch, (where you were
gold), smaller, a bit mean. People say,
Oh, you're sentimental: a dog with a dark
muzzle, a cropped tail. I recall Jesse
at the bush, the footbridge, her last year.
You're gone. Reverend Jackson is still here,
and Garret Hongo, in whose poem a man

came from Taiwan, only to be gunned down
outside a laundromat, a Chicago sidewalk.
Hongo the mentor, Hongo the master
says, Let me tell you so you won't forget
the man's dropped bag of laundry, glazed
eyes. Do you remember, entity out of time,
an hour? An arching footbridge, Jackson's
run, Hongo's "The Legend," life on earth?

Machias

In a low ceiling building in Camp Tien Sha
Rich called Sandi. "I only had a few beers."
I didn't get on the phone and say hi. Rich
was having a private moment in public, it
was kind of a big deal to make a phone call.
I never did my year in Danang. I don't recall
ever seeing Rich Cappa after that night
which was shortly after I got to Vietnam.

He was there before I. He and Sandi I, that
phone call was a Sunday night in August.
I met them a Sunday night in July a week
after I'd been in Machias, upstairs rooms
Sandi was there, dark bangs, dark eyes,
a face shaped like a tragedy-comedy mask.
We drank beer that night, too, six-packs,
and quarts of Big Cat malt liquor, six of us

upstairs in a house on a hill on a corner.
We'd driven in from the base in Cutler where
Rich, either a radar or radio tech, stood
watches. I lived there but don't recall Rich,
his perfect square face, the cleft in his chin,
standing watch, as did others, the Cappas'
that night. I saw Sandi only a few times.
In the fall she moved back to San Diego.

In the barracks at Cutler Rich lived rent-free.
We were government property. I've no gripe
about that. Had I tried at Camp Tien Sha
to make a call I could have. After I'd been
at Cutler a few months, taking the liberty
bus into Machias: Helen's restaurant (still
there), the old theater with its marquee,
a steepled church, a college on a high hill,

Main Street itself a winding hill, I brought
a 58 powder-blue Impala there, way up fifty
miles east of Ellsworth. I wonder if Sandi
wore bangs that night Rich called her, if
she sat at a counter in a kitchen. What time
of day or night it was. The beer hall where
Rich and I drank was crowded. We crossed
a wide street. Mostly I miss Machias.

Pets

Why should I care?

Because pets are good people
Because pets aren't people
Because pets mess things up
And must be cleaned up after
Because pets are not boring
Not complicated
Though each is different
Pets are not indifferent
They are not virtual they are real
Their coats limbs muscles
Eyes mouths ears and hearts
Pets feel and express feelings
They obsess but not like humans
Complain but not like humans
They misbehave they don't lie
If you treat a pet well
The pet will treat you well
They can be taught they are smart
They don't have cards and accounts
They have food and water
They have you

Permian Basin

I live in a basin.
There are no trees.
I look out at where earth meets sky.

No window to look out at a river.
I stay here, I don’t live here. I live
a mile from Ed’s Manor Tavern,

a stone throw from the lumberyard
on Madison and River,
in a house by woods

and a river. Lots of trees.
This basin, my mother
would think another world.

are chaste. You have to be pretty chaste,
clean, to be a nun, really clean to be a nun
that sails from Ireland to Ellis Island
and in Fort Lee starts Holy Angels girls
Catholic high school. Since I can't come up
with chaste's opposite, corrupt? I'll say dirty.
You have to be pretty dirty to be a vamp,
a priestess of seduction and corruption
in decadent Hollywood, a vamp, a femme
fatale, Dona Sol in the famed silent *Blood
and Sand.* I'm thinking of Nita Naldi, niece
of the Holy Angels (that my sister attended)
founder. Mary Dooley, aka Nita Naldi went
there too, and dropped out. From what I
know Mary was born in an East Side slum,
three siblings died when infants, she was
orphaned at fourteen, but I guess looks,
talent, luck and something, the hand of
God? driving the inner Mary, landed her in a
studio, modeling, then in a chorus line, then
in silents being filmed in Fort Lee. Fort Lee
was Hollywood before Hollywood was
Hollywood. How'd she ever find time and
energy, with all the rickets and scurvy of the
East Side slum, to sit behind a desk in her
aunt, her great aunt's school. The great
aunt's order was the Dominicans. They

wore, like other nuns, wimples, also habits that resembled shields you'd see on official signs, with lions to the left/ right and coming to a point at the bottom, only Dominicans' habits came to a point at the top. They were big, so when you saw one you knew this is a nun, a bride of Christ, a clean person. In *Blood and Sand*, Valentino is Juan, Spain's matador, their top notch man with the sword and cape in the bullring.

Yes, he's gored, but ultimately dies for love. Lila Lee plays the wife/ widow, Nita Naldi the other woman, maybe in life, the other woman too. They lived hard and fast, vamps. In one photo, the curve of a hip, Naldi's back gets the spotlight, you don't see her face. Her dark hair bobbed, her pale back, curves lovely to look at, and desire? She's wearing a sheet. You know that's all she's wearing.

Washington Senators

Whose autograph would you rather have, Albert Einstein
or Taylor Swift?
Pedro Ramos, a pitcher,
ran the fastest of any in the Majors.

His cursive scrolls across blue-lined paper;
his thin, curvy lips, good eyes, light brown hair,
a contrast to swarthy Camilo Pascual, the better pitcher.
Both are Washington Senators, the American League cellar.

Pedro about to board a bus outside Yankee Stadium,
the sky overcast, I hand him pen and paper,
see his signature. He and Camilo raised in Batista's Cuba,
Pascual is the Senators' ace. My friend Ray

Birmingham, a renowned coach, could tell you their best pitches.
The name's letters glide above a blue line, Ramos glides
across outfield grass, timed, faster than all other pitchers.
I lost the autograph,

the paper in folds, that lay on a walnut end table.
Who won that day? Ray could tell me about the '57 Senators'
starters. Pascual already on the bus,
my life and Ramos's collide.

L & M

I'm not taking about the cigarettes,
I'm talking about matriarch patriarch,
matriarch Lena Younger from Lorraine
Hansberry's soul, and the Platonic matador
in bullring earth. Lena said we're a family
who gives life. The matador's sword gleam
cape wave death family adore the sword
thrust stops the bull's heart. Lena Younger

says who gives life on stage to Ruth,
Beneatha, Travis, you and me. Her Chicago
apartment illusion, in reality she's on stage.
Similarly, the bullfight is not a fight.
Either the bull's going to kill the matador
or the matador the bull an illusion of war
since, against the matador, when it comes
down to fact, the bull is defenseless.

That bull, one in the stands says, is a fighter.
An illusion. Look at the admiring crowd's
fixation on the cape wave, sword thrust
takes skill, bravery. The bull slain
for entertainment, Barcelona could be
anywhere, the bull a Platonic bull killed
for a thrill. Similarly Lena's audience isn't
just Ruth, her son, her sister-in-law wants

to be a doctor, Lena, mother of pent up
Walter Younger; her audience is us.
We see the life in her eyes, hear
her declaration. We either do or don't.
In Caracas I almost went to a bull fight,
in a room I saw Lena on film, and heard
words Hansberry set down for all time.
The matador's heart, nothing next to hers.

Schaeffer and the Straight Line

Everyone had a ruler to make straight lines.
Mr Z an English teacher, Carl
a good neighbor, a handwriting expert,
enjoyed flying a kite. Mr. O' Shaughnessy
blind in one eye since childhood
from a BB gun. Also, Miss Desmond,
her ruler on paper, drew straight lines
before and after playing piano
for kindergarteners. Mr. Baldwin,
a ruler in his briefcase, walked out the door
one morning, never to be seen again.
People Schaeffer knows,
some flesh and blood, others ghosts.
More have held rulers than rosary beads,
bows, automatic rifles and slingshots.
More owned rulers than cars,
more handled rulers than flew in airplanes.
Think of rulers on desks of secretaries,
on desks of sellers of furniture and motor
vehicles. Fewer rulers now than five, ten,
fifty years ago. They were very popular.
Though there doesn't seem less a demand
for straight lines now than then.
No one says, Oh, we make straight lines
without rulers. Now,
lines are more on screens than on paper.
Screens do more than keep out flies.
Fifty years ago people walked up
to a TV to turn on the screen.

There was the big screen of Hollywood
stars, rulers in silents and talkies.
School was a splintery, warped floor,
rows of students at ink well desks.
Burly Mr. O'Shea came down and hit
Michael Phelan's hand with the ruler.
It didn't seem to hurt.

Just for You

In one of my “favs,”
Steve Wilson and the Red Caps,
we have “Here on earth
and up above.” Up above, the sun,
day after day after day, at night the moon
or just dark.
Let’s go around the block, an arc
that gradually comes down to where I am:

the lady like Washington on the dollar bill
peeks from lace curtains;
Mrs B’s younger son rock-n-rolls;
Mrs F suffers
a cerebral hemorrhage in a dentist’s chair;
Mrs E saves my ass from a nest of yellow jackets;
Mr F, swarthy in gray works his ass off;
Mrs R, the lady on the Sunkist Raisins box’s
double is next door to
Mr B, the road department, who’s next door to
Mr M, electricity; Mr E sun-visor,
lumberyard lights and shadows giant,
knuckles gnarled by rheumatoid,
mows grass,
a mower he doesn’t turn on, just pushes—

they’re not all up there smiling down.
Mr R, trench-coat, a valise swings light
in his left hand. His key
unlocks a door. Home, sweet home.

Were I Steve Wilson
of Here on earth and up above's
"Just for You,"
I'd praise oak shade on a hill
a Schwinn on a kickstand,
a garage's raised door.

Leftovers

Resentment looks like sausage links,
sauerkraut, potato salad on a paper plate
on a picnic bench, a warm day, flies
buzzing. You want to dump the plate
in a barrel but don't want to walk a hundred
yards. There are flies, germs, yellow jackets.

If resentment looks like anything
the sauerkraut stands out.
You like sauerkraut but not leftover,
with flies. You found the plate, stumbled
on it in this sparse park in Lake Village,
where there's no more or less resentment
than in Star City or any other delta town.

Look at this mess on a paper plate.
You can't help but look, you chose to be
in this park that has only a few benches
and one trash barrel. You chose to come
to Lake Village, enter its school, tell
the kids about poems, have them write.
Your partner David Reveal propped
his feet on the desk as you recited a poem.
He chose to be here, too.
You stopped at the park,
the paper plate, and couldn't resist
the leftovers, or who left them there.

Convent

The nuns were lesbians, the good side
they never showed, Sisters of Charity.
I never saw, tucked under accordion-like
pleats of a habit so much as a strand
of hair, much less Sister John's long lovely

nose nestle baby faced Sister Gerard's hair
or God forbid John's fingers down by
that other hair. Never saw Sister Carmella's
tongue in Sister Infante's mouth in heat
of passion in a back pew of our church

where I liked smelling incense drifted from
a brass cup's lid. Never saw Margret,
the eldest, naked, white wrinkles in her face
and her eyes behind specs was all I saw.
Faces framed in square white pleated habits

and lots of flowing black, though I could tell
if one was hefty and, oh yes, Infante's
smooth strong red hands. She loved U.S.
history and the piano. Did those hands
at night clasp Sister Michael's shoulders?

Did those lips lightly kiss Michael's waist?
I'd been studying the red pamphlet-like
book with Latin, weeks on end. Gerard
for something I did, banished me from Altar
Boys. I never stood on the altar holding

the chalice. Forgive and forget. No problem,
as we say. But what I can't forgive is I never
saw the good side, the we are women
sexual as any calendar pin up or helpmeet.
It was always the long flowing black, black

shoes with thick heels like my neighbor
Terry's gran wore when she came to visit.
I heard praying but no panting, though
the panting happened behind closed doors,
Sister Regina's device in Sister Carmella's

pretty, moments after Carmella showed her
pretty with a little hair around it, lovely to
kiss and caress, lovely to God and all
creation, their getting it, in an upstairs room,
an inner sanctum. God bless the convent.

Duel in Weehawken

Hamilton and Burr, instead of pistols
arm wrestle to resolve matters.
Pistols. No issue's worth that risk.
I wonder if Burr lost any sleep.
What'd you do?

How was your day? I killed Hamilton.
Yet Hamilton's on the ten spot.
He and Burr, the U.S. Vice
President, stepped ten paces,
turned and fired.

Where was Hamilton hit?
There's a past in cast iron fine print
marks the spot. A plaque
on a palisade overlooks the Hudson
they crossed.

Weekday mornings I winded my way
to a toll lane then into the Tunnel.
Back to the tragic duel,
Burr's better shot.
Manhattan had outlawed duels.

Donald Goines

He had a really lucid essay on injustice,
about Black people getting screwed over
by the bail system. It wasn't a rant, clear,
ordered, it made me think, he's dead right.

He was always dead right, a prophet really
for troubled times in cities, carjacking,
mugging, armed robbery, much of it done
by people strung out. He knew that life.

He could have inherited his father's dry
cleaning business. But he went in the army
and in Japan got stung out. Anyone wants
to preach the nightmare of strung out

should read one of his novels, *Black Girl
Lost* the one title comes to mind.
But he had many, and that his murder til
this day is unsolved, is tragic. He died,

literally, at the typewriter, someone broke in
to his apartment and shot him,
some paid assassin. He'd made enemies.
Try as he did, he couldn't shake the life.

A croaker before that word was popular,
in prison he read Iceberg Slim and wrote.
He could have gone to a good college.
Self-taught he lived what he wrote and he

wrote well. *Dopefiend* has a passage:
a young woman hangs herself on a shower
rack in a motel bathroom. It's riveting.
The ugly truth of what drugs did to her.

What drugs did. He had a choice,

more so than the woman whose life ended
in a restroom. He and his father died
only a month apart. Only his father,

of natural causes. Pimp, junkie, storyteller,
Black man, he wrought true fiction,
a world happening far from the tidy house
set back from the white picket fence.

Gardol

Brush with Colgate,
Colgate's gardol sounds slick.
What it is, sodium.
As hefty palm fronds sway in the sky
a net divides players.
One lifts a racquet and serves a ball
that bounces off an invisible shield.
It never gets to the net's other side.
Gardol guards all.
It shields our teeth from decay
and us from harm.
It acts in our lives like a sheet of fiberglass
only we don't lug it around.
Gardol guards us like the Diety.
God isn't fiberglass or sodium.
Invisible, intangible
God is the whirl of wind in the palms
above the court
in the 1958 commercial
for Colgate's dental cream.
A man in whites in the foreground
says Brush with Colgate.
What is God?
Not the wind but a shield
more than sodium, fiberglass.
The speaker from back then
is in God's arms
or ashes or food for worms.

Calais

Stationed at a place listed on official forms
as US NavSta Cutler, a radar station
in Maine, I was assigned its commissary
store, and reported to Chief Hadler, Kenneth
Hadler, a Catholic. I imagine his asking me
if I believe in God. I don't recall exactly
where or when I told him I too was Catholic.
One Sunday I rode with Chief Hadler
and others from our station, fifty miles
to Calais, Maine, a meeting of the Knights
of Columbus, a Catholic men's group.
It was upstairs. I barely recall that meeting.
I assume we prayed, words about the K of C
were said. Downeast Calais speaks
to the fled-but-where-to in me,
my flash in the pan, out of the way
antithesis to Bar Harbor, Kennebunkport.
I imagine Christ on a cross on a wall,
watching over us that Sunday afternoon
my only K of C meeting. I was eighteen.
Now, seventy-five, an agnostic who leans
more toward atheism than religious faith,
I remember Chief Hadler smoked cigarettes
but not what brand. I see him in kaki
shirt and slacks, a cap with a gold anchor
insignia above its black visor.
Being in Calais, a city of brick and wood,
was like walking in a giant's wooden leg.

Cape Man

Sal Agron was the Cape Man,
only he wasn't a man. Sixteen,
he stabbed two teenagers

in '59, his story
in news pages spread on a stone floor.
Fish guts soaked the paper.

Robin's gran cleaned trout.
On a breezeway
light shone through jalousies. Sal's

dark pompadour crested his pale brow.
His long, straight nose led him astray.
Her hand turned the blade.

From the Old Country,
she came to the States
with her husband, lived with her

daughter, son-in-law,
two grandkids. I wonder if Sal,
in jail, left a daughter.

Under an oak Robin's gran
taught me not to walk on my toes.
The brown bun threaded with gray

at the top of her head resembled a pin
cushion. Stout, she wore specs.
Her hands held long needles,

crocheting wool.
She sliced down skin, opening trout.
Their insides soaked Sal's cape.

Snapper

Rain falls in needles in the river,
thin as needles in a gun
in a tattoo parlor
forming on skin a snapper.

The snapper rears its head.
Black shell
of zigzag edges,
it crawls, leaves claw tracks
in blue-black silt of the riverbank.

The river curves. Trees on both sides,
the willow
across the water, a rain-gatherer.

My Reverie

I never thought about Bea Kettlewood
and she never thought about me.
I've no recall of her looking
over my shoulder
down at whatever I was drawing
or painting on the thick sheet of paper
that lay on the long table:
a face or figure or cluster of trees
on a riverbank; but that did happen.
We were in her room to draw and paint.

I recall the long windows' view of
dense woods behind a barbed wire fence.
Dark even in sunlight, deep shade.
No one went in there.
Out the windows, the woods stood
across the hilly street, fenced in, dark.
The room always light, at one long table
sat Raiden with her teased blonde hair
and Martha, taller, more slender,
teased black hair. Raiden wasn't chubby.

Like Martha she had a nice shape. They
were together so much I can't think of one
without the other. Raiden and Martha,
blonde and brunette, and Mrs. Kettlewood's
salt and mostly pepper hair, bowl-cut,
bangs like a monk's.
Her hair and black-framed glasses made
her look like a woodchuck.
I never thought that then, never thought
about her, but she was there, as was Estelle

whose hair was long and dark, just a shade
lighter than Martha's, but never teased.
Estelle's came down past slender shoulders.
She was tallish, thin, with olive skin.
Her dark, very dark eyes lit up my world
all of me. I believed in her eyes
nose, cheekbones, jawline, chin, sensuous
shapely mouth. Her long face, not too long.
Her thin body I thought willowy, graceful,
as she sat at a table, as she got up and

walked in the room. Something else, she
was. Raiden and Martha were lovely girls,
friendly, never flirty, at least not with me.
They were older, where Estelle was younger
by a year, than I. When you're fifteen,
as I was, fourteen's much younger.
I've ever felt about anyone more intensely.
Estelle's gone from this world ten years
and those feelings are still here.
She was, is so lovely, graceful, willowy.

I had a crush like you wouldn't believe.
To kiss Estelle would have been paradise,
my "dream come true," and it did, one night,
one night only, but that's another story.
What happened in that room was one day
we were both standing in one corner.
She said, "Why aren't you talking to me?"
I had a funny way of showing I liked her,
talking to Martha, Raiden, to others, but
not to her. I forget my mumbled reply.

Should have said, "I'm not talking to you
because I love you. You are the most
beautiful human being I have ever seen.
Your beauty..." confounded me,
so, for a while, I showed
my love for her in my silence. Here
I am trying to make sense of it. What folly!
I recall "Why aren't you talking to me?"
Estelle's voice quiet, breathy. Her eyes.
She had a way of speaking with her eyes.

Notecards

"Boobs in a church." What did you say?
"Boobs in a church." The frat boy
in the front row looked at me, I at him.
Monday night, Freshman Comp. I'd passed
out nouns in magic marker: umbrella/
courthouse; rabbit's foot/ tunnel; wallet/
gym. Boots/ church, her prompts.
From the back, her high-pitched voice,
boots sounded different. A slim neck,
hair pulled up, dark eyes, flawless skin,
petite, shapely, she had to be there
as did I, if I wanted a paycheck. Spring,
April. Fountain pen/ swimming pool.
A stolen pen, the pool members only.
Tennis racquet/ nightclub; penguin/ ring.
There were animal cards. In an open door,
Saturday morning, mortgage-free, two
baths newly remodeled, I wonder where
she is. Outside our room, *Discover*
the Last Frontier, an astronaut tiny in
a galaxy poster on a board. The astronaut
helmet comes back silver. How did I get here?
How does anyone, where they are?
Toothbrush/ stadium. Wilbur brushes his
teeth in the bleachers. Fourth quarter
fervor. He clutches the wrong end.
In his hand, soggy bristles. A buzzer
sounds. A ball bounces off a rim. Crest
clouds the water in his red cup. His
Nighthawks walk off the court, their third
consecutive loss. Two other cards,
mirror/ cemetery, belong to a Suns fan.

Against Torture

We should take them
and put them in little black boxes
for a while, each day.

But that's torture. We are a county
against torture.

On a sunny day I was in a little black box.

But you were only there fifteen maybe
twenty minutes.

The number of days per week, the length
of time per day depends on the crime,
the criminal. If the abuser thew a cat into
a tub of scalding water,

we should put that person in a box
so pitch dark they see only what's
in their mind, and barely move
knees and elbows.

That's torture. We do not torture.

But look what they did.

The Day After the Day the Music Died

I have a diary entry about Buddy Holly,
Richie Valens and J.P. Richardson, aka
The Big Bopper. I remember the classroom's
rickety wood floor. I'm keen on hardwood
floors but this floor lacked gloss. Still,
it's what I recall best about that room,
where I learned about the plane crash
then went home and wrote about it.

Art Costello's brother came in
one morning in boots, jeans, shirtless
with a crop of dark hair spilled down his
brow and in his hand a brown paper bag,
Art's lunch, he handed to Sister John at
her desk up front. A long pole's hook
opened and closed windows, we were
at basement level, the girl's playground

east of where we sat. My diary is green,
diamond-pattered, with a dark blue spine,
a latch for a key lost years ago.
I can open it and find what I wrote that day.
I remember Sister's face, Art's
close-together features made him older
and worried. His brother came in shirtless
on a warm day. We were all startled.

It was quick, quiet, nobody said anything.
He was muscled but not overly so. His
hair spilled over like Richie Valens' hair.
I'd seen Richie, Buddy and The Big Bopper
but only on TV. Clean-cut Buddy Holly
always wore a tie. Our wood floor
was uneven, a level below the playground.
Word of the crash went 'round our room.

Bundy

An infant he sucked my nipple as I lay
in the hospital. Fifteen, single.
I lived two years in Mrs. Eliot's home,
then I met and married Steve, Ted
came home, and we, Steve and I
gave him a younger brother and sister.

Our eldest, handsome, affable,
grades good enough for law school,
I was proud, someday maybe for Ted
my firstborn, politics. Today I sit
in court with others, in Florida. Ted,
his own defense lawyer, wears a suit,

a bow tie. I slap the prosecutor hard
across the mouth, at least in my mind.
My blood boils how he lies:
the VW bug, the cast-crutch sympathy
seduce. A hammer-rope rape kit,

jail escapes, a twelve year old victim,
the sorority rampage, bludgeoned
by this subhuman savage. Sex
with the dead, the victims' mothers
families in court, as I am, weeping, only
my child is here, his own attorney.

Ted worked a suicide hotline. A clerk
at a law firm, nothing amiss. In jail
yesterday, in a jailhouse jumpsuit,
he leaned across a table and looked
in my eyes. I didn't do it, Mother.

As Love Goes

I loved a basketball player,
Shay, I called her, she called herself.
Shalonda. An unremarkable student
in my classes, an unremarkable player,
her team less than stellar.
In a room with computers hulked along
walls, a girl said, You come to our games,
we go to your classes, started the whole
shooting match, my Shay love.
Was it love? Sure as I'm setting down
words, and she loved me.

I sat at a desk, picked up a phone's receiver
and took her call, a day frazzled with
papers. I could have…effusive, more
talkative, warmer. I miss the warmth that is
uniquely Shay, the light in her eyes,
her face thin, dark, her stature tall, lanky,
on the short side of tall, not quite six feet.

What do I miss? Her warmth.
I miss her eyes, her angular face,
her loose stride in a hall, on a campus.
I miss mostly her loving me,
which took the shape of my reeling her in.
She was 18, 19, far from her home in Flint,
the day she and her friends were sorry
for my loss, my mother dead and buried.
My team, those girls, unruly I ruled, you go
to our games, we come to your classes.
I gave Shay my all, not enough,
as love goes.

In the snack bar she sat beside me,
a long arm around my shoulder, that day
I'd come back from my mother.

One night, a game, Shay in a scuffle,
I felt like flying out of the stands
but stayed where I was.

On the phone I could have been more
than a man at a desk strewn with papers.
In the two years I knew her, I rarely saw her
with a man, or romantic with anyone, always
with her girls, jostling near a fountain, and
in class Shay between two of her team.

A computer screen lights, her long fingers
tap keys, the room is silent, I'm up front,
the door open at a crack. I miss her.

At the Rainbow

The invisible man plants a kiss on the forehead
of absence.
Anne Evelyn Stewart can't recall
that kiss, or the name of her sister Jeanne.
"Two eggs over easy and dry rye toast,"
Jeanne tells the server.
Anne looks out a window at a traffic light
on Hargrove Road.
Seated nearer the window
she notices the chrome Harley
parked beside a silver Kia SUV.
Her eyes go to the register near the Rainbow's
front door.
A woman two booths away lifts a mug
that has a rainbow logo:
a green, yellow, orange arc on its side.
She lowers the mug. Her sandy hair
is short and neat.
Her blue tank-top says Surfing. The sugar
on Anne's French toast looks like a first
snowfall. Jeanne gets up to let Anne out
out of the booth. Princess Snowfall
is summer fall said fast,
Anne thinks as she goes to the Ladies.
"What makes you think I'm not okay? she
says aloud to herself.
In the stall a crude arrow below the name
Joey etched as if by a pin
mars one wall. The door latch is silver
and locked. Anne has no words for door
and latch.
She sits there, wanting out,
not knowing how.

Midnight

Country Kitchen in Sayreville sits off I 50,
an isle of green cuts though four lanes
out the window. In 1970 I saw a dead horse
in such an isle only it was winter, Minnesota.
In Sayreville's new Animal Wellness Center
an hour ago a lady and a guy took dogs
on blue, ribbon-thin, taut leashes through
a door: Princess, Mack and Midnight. Mack

the only one who went willingly, three dogs
I had named, counted on me. I've taken two
bites from the sausage patty on my plate
of biscuits and gravy. All I see is Midnight,
born from a moment a lab mounted a Saint
Bernard, or visa versa. You came to me
to be saved and I led you to death, turned
you over to the lady, and you looked at me.

Kathryn said, Marty, we have to be here,
we couldn't stay where we were, better here
with the County funding. Yes, it's climate
controlled. So was Fort Hamilton in Brooklyn
the day I took an oath, April, 1966, to serve
my country. My Princess, Mack, Midnight,
I took an oath and betrayed you, betrayed
myself. Kathryn was there. "We had to do it."

Had to kill off three old ones so there's room
for the others we brought here, to stay in
cages, with the others, the County dogs.
I'm director of Sayerville Pets in Need. Our
old place, when we had a hard rain, flooded.
Now, this new facility, winter-warm,
summer-cool, dry. No electric bill to pay.
West Texas, we take care of stray animals.

I can't touch the biscuits. I'm thinking of
the dead horse I saw from a Greyhound
outside Mankato. Midnight looked right into
my eyes, not wanting to budge. He knew,
animals know. They can take these biscuits
and gravy to the dumpster out back, a stray
will find some that's spilled over. A pickup
blows by on I 50, a black lab in its bed.

Should be law against that. I should be
with those three that were mine to keep
till we could adopt them out, they never had
any interest. Three old dogs. It's as if I'd
stopped my pickup and Midnight ran up,
and I gave him food and water by the side
of the road, and in the cab, shifted into first
telling myself he lives on a nearby ranch.

Hachiko

The Akita walked to the Shibuya station
with professor Ueno, each day,
each day at the station waited for Ueno's
return. One day Ueno didn't return,
Hachiko waited nine years.

So at least he made himself a legend
of loyalty. People near the station
gave him treats, petted him. Even a dog
statue there in his memory,
his story in films the sentimental watch

with a box of Kleenex nearby. Give Hachiko
a moment before turning away.
He earned it. Though he's no longer there
at the station, to feel your fingers
scratch behind his ears.

So easy to pull a Kleenex from box,
watch the credits and then get ready
for your dental appointment,
or a round of golf or a dock
where on a forklift you take pallets

into and out of trucks at Star Distributing,
or sit at a desk in a bank.
That memory of Hachiko buried
in a stack of papers that comprise
a to-do list, one: buy Lady a collar

at Pet Sense. Maybe you have
in addition to Lady, Duke (two mutt rescues,
and Midnight, a cat, a third rescue).
Your hands full, no room for more pets.
While Hachiko rescued himself,

his heroic deed, simply to live, makes
possible, not a memory,
(he died in 1935), but our knowing he
lived, if only for a moment,
before turning to other things.

Art

Paint the island in the middle of the lake
with brushes and easel and think:
at her deathbed, you became her husband.

If not for that you might be in a shelter,
a few dollars in your pocket. Your sculptor
wife made sure that this late morning,

the light just right, you can paint trees
or an abstract, its source the island, all
in how you see it. She'd had an operation
and swam at the YWCA.
You squeeze oil from a tube onto a canvas
strokes fill. Gently you kissed her brow.

My War Was in the War

My war was in the mess hall where I learned Martin Luther King, Jr. was struck down by an assassin's bullet in Memphis, Tennessee. My war was in a bunker lined with sandbags at Bridge Cargo, at night outside the bunker looking down the long Shell Road. My war was in shadows of barracks watching a sailor, Jack Lockhart who had on one forearm a colorful parrot and on the other a geisha in a long dress. Her eyes peaked over a fan, as Lockhart boxed sailor after sailor. None beat him in our camp near the China Sea. I stood watch at Bridge Ramp as forklifts drove in and out LSTs anchored dockside. My war was at Twenty Dui Tan, a house in the suburbs of Danang, a Naval Intelligence Office. Outside one night I saw a Vietnamese man who'd been on a motorbike lying in the street, injured critically by a grenade. My war was bad things happening around me. Sheldon, a guard at Museum Pier, crouched under a stone bench, his hands at his helmet to drown out mortar thuds, or try to, when the jeep patrol found him there. My war was 101 Doc Lap, an employment place with an iron gate. People in ragged attire and conical hats struggled against the force of water, hoses turned on to keep these people from passing through that gate. My war was a tower looking over a rice paddy where, the night of Tet, many had died. Looking over that paddy before and after that firefight. My war was the letters SP in white on a dark blue helmet, and the black stock of an M 16. My war was the war of many others, Vietnamese, American, Korean, who were not in the jungle but in the city of Danang and on its outskirts. The sun rose and set over Marble Mountain and the China Sea. My war was Vietnam, my war was a few get rich and many die. It was a Black GI carried in a straitjacket from a boat at a ferry launch. My war was what I had a hand in, sometimes called a conflict, my war in war. My war was all wars.

Until You Came Along

The unimaginable nothing, not the nothing I
had, a nothing with breath, a door,
a sky, a four-door burgundy Highlander.
At a florist's I wired roses for your birthday.

How enthralled I was seeing you
on a screen, our online time, face to face,
hearing you, touching. My fingers lace
a plum corset with you in it—only virtual.

Buds opened on a table near your pipe
for weed. Till you came I lived. A battery
in my SUV, a winter road, gray skies.
Then, across a counter a florist swiped

my card. I tapped keys. You appeared,
my everything, not the nothing of the dead.

Obit

He was dead most of his life,
although he didn't know it,
and by the time he was a father he died.
Not old, he raised Diane and Margaret
from infancy to adolescence.
Proud they were involved in karate
he drove them to lessons.
They kicked and lunged, lean
in white smocks. It was what he wanted,
being a father. Before they were born
he wanted others: methadone,
coke, grass. He provided others
with such things, and wanted them
to see him in the car with the girl
and drugs. Eventually he married
a girl, a nurse. He wanted a roof
for shelter, steady employment,
say, behind a bar. For he was good
mixing a Tom Collins. These girls,
first one, two years later the other.
Then he began to live, as if the self
he'd been, on a corner waiting,
looking to sell acid or score a bag of smack,
as if he never existed.

Laika

Mistakes in smoking jackets, in Speedo
trunks and goggles have memories
of animals behind bars at the zoo, train
memories, cape memories of jumping off
a roof thinking they could fly. I can't jump
rope. I'm not afraid but don't like
making mistakes. My attitude,
I have an attitude, a chip on my shoulder,
is one of loving hate. I hate that l love
them, love that I hate them.
Hate the fascist whose boot heel cracks
wings of roaches, love the actor who died
saving the child in the hotel fire, though
they're not around to take the green
rose of your love into their arms.
Mistakes are like penguins in tuxedos,
dogs like Laika on Sputnik. We test them,
try them out. The mistake went way out
there and came back whole? No,
she was a stray, died after only a few hours
in orbit, WTF, for the good of humankind.
I hate mistakes. They made a mistake
sending that dog to the moon. Look
at what they're doing now in the Ukraine.
We in the United States are as screwed up
as the Russians, almost. Mistakes are like
regrets. They gave us Chekov, they took that
dog off the streets and named her Laika
to entertain the public, so little
kids could look out their windows at night
and say, Oh, Laika's up there,

a pioneer, a galaxy captain. This dog
in the end let us down. Disappointed she
didn't survive, disappointed in Laika,
we turned to the Nixon-Kennedy.
Some thought putting a dog into space
the right move. Were he alive
Chekov might have thought it was a big
mistake, a cruel experiment,
Laika's dying for Russia, for humankind.

Rescuer

You go about your days helping animals,
so many, you said, it's a teacup
in the ocean. Money helps. Mostly
their true hearts human hearts need.
You dip your teacup in the ocean.
That's something, an act of courage.

Ed's Manor Tavern

He'd been drinking at Ed's and left alone.
His Pontiac failed to make the long turn,
toppled into a culvert, no seatbelts back
then, his leg smashed, half between Ed's
and home, a Lorillard exec, heavyset, iron
gray hair, plaster cast, bulbous pitted nose.

On his breezeway soda bottles in wooden
crates, he couldn't lift one then. I liked
the colors: lime orange strawberry black
brown red yellow, a rainbow of bottled sugar
in drab but sturdy crates delivered weekly
to his door. One color clear, like water.

I Hate Authority

Parents teachers cops judges—
don't like anyone telling me what to do.

Okay, moron. Consider,
no authority, no order. There'd be chaos.
Some desperate soul slits your throat
as you sleep,
steals the Timex
off your wrist as your blood runs
in the gutter.
Authority's a good thing,
so long as its hand doesn't reach so far
as to tell you
how to button your shirt or blouse
and what to read and eat.
You're an idiot with your hatred
of authority. Then, some think
they can make you see and act differently.
They can't. I'm sorry a parent
or just something in your DNA made
your bad attitude. Music,
drugs, bullying, neglect, poverty?
Your poverty of spirit I lack.
I'm superior. I'm an asshole.
I just don't want someone barging in
and taking everything
and my life.

For Jasmeen Kaur

In late 1980s America William Horton won
a political campaign for George Bush.
Bush's opponent Governor Michael Dukakis
had released Horton, a Black man,
a convicted felon from prison.

Dukakis is soft on crime, said Bush's poster,
a Horton photo. With Horton on the streets
no one is safe. Lee Atwater, Bush's
campaign manager, thought up the poster.
A brilliant move with a racist undercurrent,

the display of Horton, disheveled, wild-eyed,
hit below the belt: Don't vote Dukakis.
Shortly after Bush became President,
Atwater's cancer flared. His diagnosis
was terminal. At his funeral Chuck Jackson

a Black man, a famed singer of soul music
sang. He and Atwater grew up
in the same Southern town, a South steeped
in segregation, racism. Jackson
at the deathbed held his friend's hand.

Selfie

"She even thinks that up in heaven
 Her class lies late and snores"
I see, it's a poem printed on a white board.
I'm with you, behind the bulk of gold
podium. All these desks. I just popped in.
While it's just you and I..see, I know
my pronoun cases. Cases, Casey.

Jose said to George, She was just a kid.
You came into her bedroom, unzipped…
the unmentionable, Jose nailed it.
A father flies across the courtroom,
a bailiff pries father fingers from Jose's
throat, but George…Score one for Jose.
It worked. I walked out a free woman.

You'd think a father...I never knew Caylee's.
What happened? You've read about
Cindy a nurse, George a doting grandpa ,
the backyard pool, the shallow grave,
Zanny the Nanny, Universal Studios,
I work there. I'm here, with you.
What's the weather like in Orlando?

Do I like chocolate martinis?
I like to party, the Orlando club scene.
I'll toast a memory, Casey Anthony,
Mother of the Year! Tone is everything.
Jose, demonstrative, emphatic,
to George, "your daughter's mouth!"
Caylee's taped corpse, Zanny the Nanny.

You've written, If you take "even"
from the first line, the poem
is no longer Cullen's classic quatrain
"To a Lady I Know." Tone, nuance.
I should write fiction. Casey Anthony,
Mother of the Year. This podium
you hide behind. All these empty desks.

While it's just you and I, let's you hold
the iPhone, there, mom of the year's
arm round prof of the year's shoulder.
Don't get that "she even thinks."
in the picture. Big smile, here at Clovis
Community College, you and me,
big smile, lie our way to the truth.

Up and Out

Champion pole vaulter Bob Richards is up,
the abandoned air base is out. Bob
Richards, not to be confused with the great
Wendy Richard of *East Enders* and
Are You Being Served?, vaults on the box
of Wheaties, breakfast of champions
and with strength, skill epitomizes Up,
as does the air base Out: lots of macadam
to venture out to where earth meets sky,

a body could walk forever runways empty
of aircraft. Cracks with weeds form
a pattern, as did Bob Richards with his up,
over the bar, down, pattern of practice to be
in the Olympics and at meets that lacked
Olympic fanfare. All it took to do that up
and over, his one aid a pole, moves me,
as does the airbase's abandon,
its lots of walk out far as the eye can see,

its horizontal, like its sky, void of gliders and
planes. Though a few years back, a glider
fell, its pilot's life lost, I heard. I wasn't there
then. I was in a room without windows,
monitoring students writing to a prompt
called Now I'm Paying for It.
Each had a different It, most, a lot to say.
I wasn't sure that prompt would work.
One by one, they stood and read aloud.

Acknowledgements

The author wishes to thank the following journals, in which these poems first appeared:

Black Poppy Review: Maiden Rock, Permian Basin
Mad Swirl: Our Daughter's Friend, Snug, Leftovers, My War Was in the War
Erothanatos: Australia, Against Torture
Academy of the Heart and Mind: Pop Culture Elegy, Washington Senators, As Love Goes
Genuine Gold: Christina
The Insurgence: About that Sunday at the Audubon Ballroom, For Jasmeen Kaur
Chewers & Masticadores: Black Beard, White Dog; Joe, Pets, Just for You, Rescuer
Yellow Mama: Elvis's Pompadour, Nuns by Nature, Calais, Bundy, Hachiko
Backwards Trajectory: Central Air
The Gorko Gazette: Duel in Weehawken
Our Day's Encounter and *Zin Daily*: The Dog No One Wants
Bardball: Mantle and Mays
BlazeVOX: Mourners at the Mound, My Reverie
A Thin Slice of Anxiety: Other Nights, Lakes, The Difference Between A and Z, Laika
The Wrath-Bearing Tree: Fist
Art Villa: Becoming Invisible, Donald Goines, Cape Man, Notecards, Ed's Manor Tavern, I Hate Authority
Book of Matches: At the Cross
Lothlorien Journal: Message in a Bottle, Selfie, Up and Out
Lowstoft Chronicle: In Memory of Major Marie Rossi-Cayton
Off Course: The Bridge of Love, Gardol, At the Rainbow
Northwest Indiana Literary Review: Machias
Quail Belle: L & M
Avant Appalachia ezine: Schaeffer and the Straight Line
BOMBFIRE: Convent
First Literary Review-East: Snapper
Sparks of Calliope: The Day After the Day the Music Died

Locust Candy: Midnight
Moss Piglet: Art
Beatnik Cowboy: Until You Came Along
Dream Noir: Obit

www.ingramcontent.com/pod-product-compliance
Lightning Source LLC
LaVergne TN
LVHW090530110826
845146LV00003B/1049

* 9 7 9 8 9 9 0 5 5 8 5 5 7 *